A Quiet Morning for Mum

Written by Alison Hawes

Illustrated by Leonie Shearing

My name is Jane.
This is my family.

In the morning,
my mum gets up first.
The house is quiet then,
just how she likes it.

Dad gets up next.
He likes listening to the radio
in the morning.

Mum shouts,
"Can you turn it down?
It's too loud. You'll wake the baby."

Then my big sister gets up.
She likes listening to her CD
player in the morning.

Mum shouts,
"You'll wake the baby.
Can you turn it down?"

Then my big brother gets up.
He likes watching the TV
in the morning.

Mum shouts,
"It's too loud.
You'll wake the baby."

Last of all, I get up.
I like listening to my tape
in the morning.

Mum shouts,
"It's too loud.
Turn it down.
You'll wake the baby!"

Then Dad and my big sister go out to work.

Then my big brother
and I go to school.

Now the house is quiet again.
"This is just how I like it!"
says Mum.
But then...

...the baby wakes up!